LIBERARE

EMOTIONAL EATING WORKSHOP

PART I: INTRODUCTION

In the vast tapestry of our existence, there lies a profound intricacy called our nervous system. Becoming deeply attuned to its nuances as we traverse the challenging path of recovery can significantly empower us. This understanding offers us not only the tools to cultivate an environment of safety within ourselves but also to bravely navigate the ripples of anxiety that inevitably emerge when confronted with life's multifaceted challenges.

Delving into the depth of our being, as we listen intently to our body and the myriad sensations it unfurls, we embark on a transformative journey. Through this endeavour, we gradually forge a powerful alignment between our physical and emotional realms. This alignment paves the way for a heightened emotional resilience and a fortified sense of self-worth. As a result, we open the doors wide to embrace life's many treasures: the euphoria of joy, the thrill of excitement, the innocence of playfulness, the serenity of rest, the beauty of growth, the magic of healing, and the profound bond of connection.

These are not just fleeting moments, but the very essence of what each one of us is entitled to in our lives.

The journey of mastering regulatory skills and cultivating our internal safety resources is akin to refining any great art form. It demands dedication, practice, and a sea of patience.

However, a comprehensive grasp of the basic neurobiology grants us an enlightening perspective. With this newfound wisdom, we can envelop ourselves in a blanket of self-compassion, comprehending the reasons behind our occasional challenges in relinquishing distressing and harmful behaviours.

But rest assured, armed with knowledge and determination, we will reach a point where we genuinely feel secure enough to release them into the winds of the past.

THE SCIENCE-Y BIT

In our bodies we have a family of neurons which we refer to as the "Vagus Nerve." This connects the brain stem to lots of different places in our face and body and is part of the autonomic nervous system (ANS). This system controls specific body functions such as our digestion, heart rate and immune system. This is involuntary/automatic, meaning we can't consciously control them.

The ANS is divided into two parts;
- the sympathetic nervous system which tells the body to speed up
- the parasympathetic which tells the body to slow down.

The ANS scans for cues of safety and threats of danger; it does this by listening; INSIDE to what is happening in our internal organs, OUTSIDE scanning the external environment BETWEEN the nervous systems of people around us.

It is responsible for ensuring both our needs for connection and survival are met, however it has to choose either turning towards connection OR survival/protection in any given moment. To do this it moves AUTOMATICALLY between three STATES.

Safety and connection/Within our Window Of Tolerance
Fight and flight/Hyperarousal
Freeze and fawn/Hypoarousal

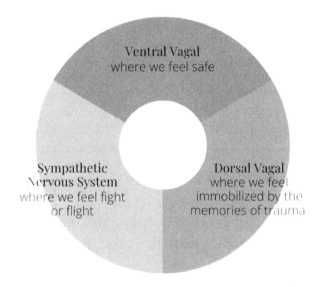

SAFETY AND CONNECTION/WOT (GREEN)

Also referred to as: Rest and digest, social engagement, regulation

Nervous system division: parasympathetic nervous system – ventral vagal complex

Feels like: Groundedness, safe, connected to self and others, mindful, in the present moment, calm, compassionate, rational, open.

Experienced as [individual]: easy breathing, lightness in the chest, clear thoughts, able to make eye contact, voice changes tone easily

Imagine: laughing with friends and family

If there is a perceived threat, the SAFETY AND CONNECTION system can become overwhelmed so the ANS will automatically change the activated state from connection to protection through firstly FIGHT AND FLIGHT, and then FREEZE and FAWN.

Threats are personal and may be anything from feeling alone, having too many responsibilities, gaining weight, an unconscious thought of being abandoned, a memory, being in a distressing relationship, getting stuck in traffic, not being able to track intake, feeling hunger, experiencing rejection.

FLIGHT AND FIGHT/HYPERAROUSAL (AMBER)

Also referred to as: Dysregulation

Nervous system division: sympathetic nervous system

The hormones adrenaline and cortisol flood the system and increase blood pressure, heart rate, fuel availability and move blood from the digestive system to the limbs.

3

Evolutionary: this supported survival by enabling us to run away from a tiger or fight a bear.
Feels like: Stress, overwhelm, anxiety, panic, fear, worry, irritation, anger, rage.

Experienced as [individual]: racing heart, shallow breathing, clammy palms, racing thoughts, unable to make eye contact, knot in belly, tension in shoulders, tight jaw

Imagine: a zebra running away from a lion, running out of a house fire

If this mobilisation of the body doesn't bring a resolution to the distress, the ANS steps down to a state of collapse FREEZE AND FAWN.

FREEZE AND FAWN / HYPOAROUSAL (RED)

Also referred to as: collapse, shutdown

Nervous system division: parasympathetic nervous system - dorsal vagal complex

Feels like: dissociation, stuck, hopelessness, increased pain threshold, no hunger cues, depression, shame, confusion, going through the motions, checked out, desire to please and appease others.

Experienced as [individual]: heaviness, sluggish, unable to move, blank thoughts, unable to make eye contact, monotone voice

Imagine: a turtle going into its shell

THEORIES

There are two main theories that look at the nervous system in this way, the The Poly Vagal Theory by Stephen Porgues and The Window Of Tolerance Theory by Dan Siegal.

Eating disorder behaviours happen outside of "Social Engagement" or "Window Of Tolerance".

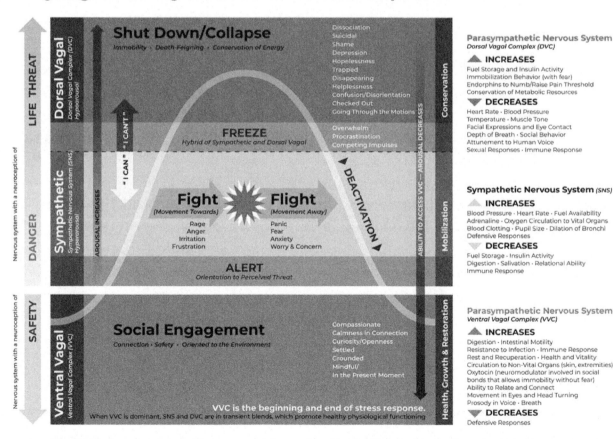

© Ruby Jo Walker, LCSW 2023 · Southwest Trauma Training · swtraumatraining.com · Adapted by Ruby Jo Walker from Cheryl Sanders, Anthony "Twig" Wheeler, and Steven Porges

WINDOW OF TOLERANCE THEORY

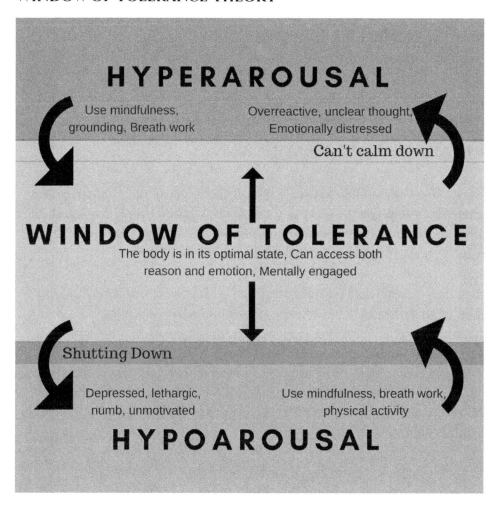

Our nervous system matters because it shapes the way we experience our life. Our behaviours, beliefs and the way our body responds are due to the state of our nervous system.

Our body and brain are interconnected, the state or our nervous system will impact our "story", the thoughts we have and how we experience daily life.

WHY IS THIS IMPORTANT?

We want to spend most of our daily lives in a state of safety and connection / within the window of tolerance so we can experience joy, happiness, excitement, healing, growth, health, learning and rest; we also want our nervous system to accurately listen and respond to real threats of danger, for example a house fire; and then move back into a state of safety and connection. We call this AUTONOMIC FLEXIBILITY.

DISORDERED EATING AND EXERCISE BEHAVIOURS

Disordered eating and exercise behaviours may have initially developed unconsciously as an effective strategy to bring about feelings of safety and connection when things felt tough or when experiencing something that may overload an already vulnerable nervous system. The behaviour of eating uses the same neural complex as safety and connection does.

For example, a child may have heard their parents arguing and felt unsafe (a threat), they may have self soothed through eating to bring a sense of grounding or numbing [parasympathetic activation = safety / freeze] to help manage dysregulation. This coping mechanism may have continued unconsciously into adulthood; however now after each binge episode when there is a realisation of the amount of food consumed, this creates panic [sympathetic activation = flight and fight / hyperarousal] and the urge to ground or numb happens again which unconsciously leads to another binge episode as they have not learnt any other way to cope and regulate.

It is not uncommon for individuals experiencing disordered eating to move between dysregulated or protection states; however in fight or flight [amber], behaviours may present as food rituals, obsessive thoughts around food, loss of appetite, digestive issues, excessive exercise or attempting to do a certain number of steps per day (flight response). Often the fight response can be observed in symptoms such as self induced vomiting, chewing and spitting, self harm behaviours and hatred or anger towards the body. In a state of freeze [red], symptoms may show up the desire to shrink or disappear, digestive issues, binge eating or extreme exercise in attempt to feel something.

Experiencing disordered eating behaviours and not feeling able to stop them, is in itself traumatic; leaving us stuck in a loop of protection and dysregulation. Any attempt to change these behaviours that once kept us safe, elicits a protective response from the nervous system; and in these dysregulated states logical thinking is impaired, which is why it may seem like we cannot reason with the "ED voice" in that moment.

Understanding this helps to offer some compassion to ourselves as to why it can be so hard to change disordered eating behaviours as it can feel like removing a safety blanket.

However, the nervous system learns through experience. This means that habitual response patterns can be interrupted and new patterns can be created. Which means that eating freely, not tracking and embracing rest can eventually feel safe through developing awareness to body based feelings, tuning into nervous system state and story with compassion, and learning and implementing skills to automatically return safely to regulation.

Ultimately, in a state of safety and connection, growth, healing and change is possible.

HEART RATE VARIABILITY

We can measure our vagal tone through heart rate variability (HRV) This can show us how healthy our nervous system is, or how much time we spend in a safe and connected state.

Heart rate tells us how many times a minute our heart beats, HRV tells us the variation in time between the heart beats. We want a high level of variability as this means that our ventral vagal complex (SAFETY AND CONNECTION) is active and we can adjust to the demands of daily life (AUTONOMIC FLEXIBILITY).

HRV measures can be found on some Garmins, Apple Watches, WHOOP bands and Oura rings.

PART 1: EXERCISE 1
Tune into your body in this moment, describe what you are experiencing. You can use these descriptors to help describe sensations;

Texture : flat, dull , rough, firm, soft, smooth, fuzzy
Weight: heavy, light, spacious, cramped, dense, deep
Pain: deep, sharp, intense, subtle, ache, chronic, consistent, irregular, moving, burning, prickly, electric
Pace: quick, slow, stagnant, strong, rapid
Temperature: hot, cold, warm, chilly, damp, frosty, clammy, airy
Vibration: tingly, fuzzy, slow, shaky, smooth, pounding, irregular
Size: tiny, small, little, giant, big, in front, behind, next to, all-consuming, taking over
Colour: red, yellow, black, multi colour, the colour of sky

From this exploration what state do you think your nervous system is in?

EXERCISE 2

At the moment, how do you know which state you are in?

Consider both the physiological state [body sensations]

And psychological story [thoughts, beliefs, feelings]

What state do you spend most of your time in?

9

Take time to go back in your memories and bring to your mind a time that you were in each state. Write down a few paragraphs about this time and give the story a name. This acts as a LANDMARK and ANCHOR for you to help start to recognise what state you are in at each moment. For example; "I feel similar sensations to when that HUGE ROW happened, I recognise this state as e.g. fight or flight".

SAFETY AND CONNECTION/wot (GREEN)

FLIGHT AND FIGHT/hyperarousal (AMBER)

FREEZE AND FAWN / Hypoarousal (RED)

EXERCISE 4

Start to recognise what makes you feel a sense of safety; we call these SAFETY CUES OR SAFETY ANCHORS; and they automatically offer respite to our nervous system.

Consider who (people, pets), what activities (e.g. walk to work, watching the sunset, read a book, watering the plants) , places (e.g by the sea, at the coffee shop, in my bedroom, in the shower), when (e.g. climbing into bed, leaving work, Sunday morning). Note all these down and add to them over time.

Start to recognise when you are in a state of safety and connection and take a moment to note down how that feels for you.

EXERCISE 5

Start to think about all the things in your daily life that feel like a threat and automatically activate the protection [fight and flight or freeze and fawn] response. Note these down and reflect on whether these are real threats to danger or survival or not.

Common ones related to disordered eating include eating a meal someone else has cooked, taking a rest day, a change in routine, experiencing high hunger levels, comparing your body to others in person or in the media, feeling like you're lazy or lack will power, etc (and beating yourself up in your head).

The aim of nervous system regulation in recovery is to treat yourself with self compassion and face challenges with confidence and resilience. To have the skills to "feel the fear, and do it anyway".

PART 2: INTRODUCTION:

Having a greater understanding about the effects of food, nutrients and eating has on the body will support offering self compassion and self tenderness when behaviours around food and eating feel out of control or scary.

When we start to see food as both fuel, and more than fuel we can offer it greater respect and thus create more space to notice how we are using it or avoiding it to help us cope with discomfort and unease.

It is important that we see health as multifactorial; to include physical, social, emotional, mental and spiritual health. When we see health this way, we can start to reframe our beliefs around food's role in our lives and how it serves us in more ways than we perhaps recognise.

NERVOUS SYSTEM OVERVIEW

The autonomic nervous system (ANS) receives information about the body and external environment [cues of safety and threats of danger]; it responds by stimulating body processes [speed up], or inhibiting them [slow down] through the parasympathetic division. The polyvagal theory suggests that the ANS moves through three states on a continuum in response to the information it receives. This happens automatically, without conscious control.

State 1: Safety and connection occurs when there are minimal threats of danger and plenty of safety cues. This may feel like regulated, calm and grounded.

State 2: If there is a perceived threat the nervous system will activate "survival/protection mode" and enter fight or flight to support the body to move away from or fight the danger by release hormones adrenaline and cortisol. This may feel like anxiety, overwhelm and stress.

State 3: If mobilisation does not bring resolution to the distress the nervous system will move into freeze and fawn in attempt to survive. This feels like collapse, immobility, dissociation and a disconnect from the body, the self and world around

When in survival mode, the brain shuts off some parts to focus on survival and protection. This means that logic and reason can be impaired. This can make it hard to reframe thoughts and beliefs.

Story follows state: the state of our nervous system will impact our thoughts and beliefs which have an impact on our behaviours.

We want to have flexible nervous systems so that we spend the majority of the time in a state of safety and connection but can move into fight, flight, freeze and fawn when there is an actual threat to our survival.

Disordered eating and exercise behaviours may have initially unconsciously developed as an effective strategy to bring about feelings of safety and connection when things felt tough. They may also be keeping us feel safe from things that do feel like a threat to us such as being in a bigger body.

Experiencing disordered eating behaviours and not feeling able to stop them, is in itself traumatic; leaving you stuck in a loop of protection and dysregulation [amber and red]. Any attempt to change these behaviours that once kept you safe, elicits a protection response from the nervous system.

Understanding this helps to offer some compassion to yourself as to why it can be so hard to change disordered eating behaviours as it can feel like removing a safety blanket. However, the nervous system learns through experience. This means that habitual response patterns can be interrupted and new patterns can be created.

SAFETY ANCHORS

As we are likely to be in a state of survival or dysregulation when we turn to disordered eating behaviours, as well as go into a dysregulated state (when we start to challenge our fears around eating or exercise), it is important that we know our current safety anchors and create more.

Safety anchors are not designed to remove the anxiety or distress but rather to make it feel more tolerable, to increase our resilience. To "feel the fear and do it anyway."
If we imagine a really stormy sea and us trying to swim in it, safety anchors and skills are designed not to make the sea less stormy, but rather for us to become stronger swimmers.

As we want to spend most of the time in a state of safety and connection it is important to know how we experience this by listening to our bodies when we are in this state. What sensations do we experience? What feelings do we have? What thoughts are we having? What behaviours are we likely to be performing? This can help us identify ways that we can return to this state.

We can create daily habits and routines that bring us more general opportunities to experience this state such as spending time in nature, non sleep deep rest, yoga, journalling, getting adequate sleep, eating enough regularly, resting and relaxing, being creative and connecting; we can also develop in the moment rituals to turn to when we are experiencing hyper/hypo arousal to support us tolerate the distress without turning to unhealthy behaviours or avoiding the challenge.

These are different for everyone and involve a bit of trial and error so it is important to see it as experimental, and note down what works and doesn't work so well.

IN THE MOMENT REGULATION EXAMPLE:

1.Three deep inhales with long exhales (Cocoa breaths).

2. Notice:
- Five things you can see
- Four things you can touch
- Three things you can hear
- Two things you can smell
- One thing you can taste.

3. Ask yourself "Am I in danger, or am I safe?".

CREATING NEW SAFETY ANCHORS

When considering new ways to establish feelings of safety, connection and regulation try exploring the below four areas to bring you back into the present moment and back into connection with the body. It is important that any new skills, interventions or techniques are practised when in a regulated state before trying to use them at a time of distress. The more practice the easier it can feel.

Using the breath: consider different types of breathwork e.g. inhaling for three and exhaling for six and repeat for five rounds, box breathing and taking two inhales followed by one long exhale.

Using movement: movement can be useful as a form of bilateral stimulation to engage the full brain. Walking is a safe form of movement if we are unsure what state we are in. If we are in a state of collapse anything too intense such as running can move us out of the state too quickly and lead us to experience intense anxiety or overwhelm. Gentle rocking, swaying or dancing can be beneficial too. If we know we are in a state of fight or flight then we can perform a more intense movement such as running or shaking to discharge the anxious energy.

Engaging the senses: our senses can be a useful tool to help us return to the body. It can be useful to come up with a list of things we feel might be soothing and try these; consider things to look at, things to smell e.g. candle or scented hand cream, things to touch e.g. cosy blanket, warm mug, warm shower, things to taste e.g. cup of mint tea and things to listen to e.g. calming music.

Connection: we can use the people and pets around us to support us to co-regulate. This works both ways, so we may often feel more stressed or excited when the people around us are stressed or excited; but if we are aware of the people in our lives that are calming influences we can try to spend more time with them.

FOOD AS NOURISHMENT

When we reframe the act of eating food as nourishment for the body, mind and spirit we offer ourselves a way of understanding why we may turn to food when we are not physically hungry or why we restrict it when we are.

PHYSICAL NOURISHMENT

Food nourishes us by providing our bodies and minds with energy and nutrients. When in recovery from any type of disordered eating we want to be able to meet our body's physical needs. We can do this by ensuring we are eating in structured, yet flexible, way. We all have individual needs but what often works well is eating three meals and three snacks daily, avoiding going for longer than three to four hours in between eating episodes.

When we are not consuming adequate intake regularly this can reduce blood glucose levels; this can feel like a threat to the nervous system, pushing it into protection mode and triggering disordered eating behaviours. We want to avoid spending excessive time thinking about food or over planning but what is beneficial is to create a flexible weekly plan.

EMOTIONAL AND MENTAL NOURISHMENT

Food nourishes us emotionally in multiple ways. Firstly it does this by balancing our blood glucose. If we are not eating regularly and this causes big dips or elevations in our blood glucose this often creates changes in our mood; by ensuring we consume mixed meals in a structured way across the day can prevent mood swings.

We can also utilise food as a coping mechanism when emotions feel too big to cope with. Emotional eating is normal and not something we need to feel ashamed of.

The act of eating can be cathartic as it engages the safety and connection pathway (which is often referred to as rest and digest) by engaging the senses, creating a rhythmic motion and opening the jaw. It can be helpful to tune in before engaging in emotional eating to try to understand what we are trying to get from food, what need we are trying to meet; it is important to do this with curiosity and not judgement. Emotional eating can become distressing if it is the only coping tool in the toolbox.

Certain nutrients can also support the health of the brain and nervous system and thereby support our hormones and neurotransmitters to function better. Including fatty acids in the diet is especially important, especially omega 3's.

Try to include oily fish at least twice per week. Oily fish includes salmon, tuna steak, as well as mackerel and trout.

Other nutrients to consider are:
Iron as lack of iron can lead us to feel weak, tired and lethargic. Foods rich in iron include red meat, poultry, fish, beans and pulses and fortified cereals.

B vitamins: Not getting enough B1, B3 and B12 can make you feel low, tired and irritable. Animal protein foods such as meat, fish, eggs and dairy, and fortified cereals are rich in B vitamins.

Folate: When you don't get enough folate you can be at a higher risk of feeling low in mood . Folate can be found in green vegetables, citrus fruits, liver, beans and fortified foods like marmite.

Selenium: A selenium deficiency may increase the chance of feeling depressed and other negative mood states. Good sources of selenium include Brazil nuts, seeds, wholemeal bread, meat and fish.

SPIRITUAL NOURISHMENT

There is not a huge amount of research into the role that food plays in spiritual nourishment but we can look at it in two ways. Firstly the food we eat can help connect us with Mother Nature and with each other. We can enhance our connection by thinking and giving gratitude to all the people involved in growing, packaging, transporting and selling our foods; as well as thinking about how all parts of the food is grown, and perhaps start to grow a few vegetables of our own.

We can also try to tune into the foods that support us to feel grounded as a way to support us return to regulation if we know we are likely to be hyper aroused after a stressful situation. These are individual but may include foods that are grown in the ground such as root vegetables and potatoes, as well as warming soups, stews and casseroles. Foods that are rich in minerals may also be included here as they receive the minerals from the earth, for example seeds, nuts, avocados. Or perhaps a simple warm tea will work for us.

SOCIAL NOURISHMENT

Connecting with other people is so important for our health and happiness, as well as for creating feelings of safety and co-regulation. Connecting over food is a wonderful way to nourish our social health; whether it is a pizza with friends on a Friday night or a fajita night with the family, these rituals of meeting and greeting impact us in a hugely positive way as it enables us to share the joy. This may mean that sometimes the foods are not optimal in physical nourishment but because we are moving to see health as multifactorial we can see how these rituals and occasions are so valuable too.

PART 2: EXERCISE 1

Tune into your body in this moment, describe what you are experiencing. You can use these descriptors to help describe sensations;

Texture : flat, dull , rough, firm, soft, smooth, fuzzy
Weight: heavy, light, spacious, cramped, dense, deep
Pain: deep, sharp, intense, subtle, ache, chronic, consistent, irregular, moving, burning, prickly, electric
Pace: quick, slow, stagnant, strong, rapid
Temperature: hot, cold, warm, chilly, damp, frosty, clammy, airy
Vibration: tingly, fuzzy, slow, shaky, smooth, pounding, irregular
Size: tiny, small, little, giant, big, in front, behind, next to, all consuming, taking over
Colour: red, yellow, black, multi colour, the colour of sky

From this exploration what state do you think your nervous system is in?

EXERCISE 2

What are your current safety anchors?

When did you last use them?

How did you notice a change in state?

What are three new safety anchors you could explore this week? Consider breath work, engaging the senses and movement.

EXERCISE 3

How are you nourishing your physical health at the moment?

23

What two changes can you make to support this area further?

How will you measure your progress on this?

In what ways are your nourishing your emotional and mental health with food and nutrients?

Are you using food as a coping mechanism?

If so, does it cause you distress or guilt?

What do you think you need in that moment?

How else could you provide yourself with this?

Are you abstaining from food as a way to prevent nourishing yourself in anyway?

Explore why you think this is.

Consider how nourishment was modelled to you and how you feel about your self esteem.

EXERCISE 5

In what ways could you explore nourishing your spiritual self using food in a positive way?

What rituals could you create with food to support your social health?

The aim if seeing food as nourishment to all areas of our life can support us to reframe the negative beliefs we have been taught about food and eating and start to see it as a safer, more connecting and joyful experience.

PART 3: INTRODUCTION:

With safety resources in place it is now that we can notice and reflect upon the behaviours, feelings and physiological impact that the disordered eating and exercise has on us. These allow us to notice what we need to change and knowing these can be something to reflect back on to see how much progress has happened.

We can also look at the aspects of our lives that are enabling the disordered behaviours to continue; these are called maintaining mechanisms. Once we understand this we can reflect on the past, not to dig around there too much but to understand and accept how early life experiences and our core beliefs impact the way we see ourselves and how safe we feel the world around us is. This allows us to understand why we may have turned to eating behaviours and bring self compassion to ourselves.

FORMULATION

A formulation is commonly used in counselling and therapy, predominantly cognitive-behavioural therapies but also in other modalities. It helps us to understand the origin, current status, and maintenance of a problem and thus offers direction to focus on. Formulations are not set in stone, but rather something to amend and add to over time as we learn more about ourselves, our childhoods and become aware of our thinking patterns.

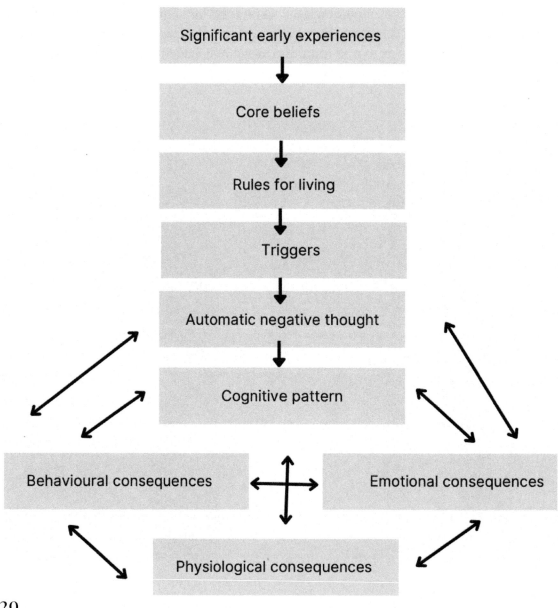

Many women find it easiest to start at the base of the formulation and work upwards. The consequences are otherwise known as the disordered or distressing behaviours being performed as well as the emotional and physiological state that are the result of them or are contributing to them. Exploring this can sometimes trigger experiences of anxiety so we need to have safety and grounding resources available.

Behavioural examples:

- Restricting food intake
- Watching "what I eat in a day" videos
- Binge eating
- Obsessively calorie counting
- Walking X amount of steps per day
- Not buying certain foods
- Avoiding social events that involve eating
- Not going swimming or wearing shorts
- Doing all the cooking in the household
- Making excuses to move more

Emotional examples:

- Anxiety
- Fatigue
- Shame
- Guilt
- Fear
- Resentment

Physiological examples:

- Loss of menses
- Fatigue
- Bloating
- Constipation
- Insomnia
- Inflammation

These are otherwise referred to as thought distortions and are habitual errors in thinking which have developed over time as a way to protect the self and remained in place causing inaccurate thoughts.

Types of Distortions:

Women tend to recognise a couple of distortions that they commonly find themselves reverting too, a few example are:

- Black and white/all or nothing thinking : this distortion happens when people think in extremes
- Overgeneralisation: this occurs when an individual reaches a conclusion about one event and then incorrectly apply that conclusion across the board.
- Catastrophising: this type of thinking leads people to dread or assume the worst when faced with the unknown.
- Personalisation: this occurs when someone takes something personally when it is not connected in any way.
- Mind reading: this occurs when someone assumes they know what someone else is thinking
- Mental filtering: the tendency to ignore positives and focus exclusively on negatives.
- Labeling: this occurs when people reduce themselves or other people to a single characteristic

Noticing triggers

Bringing awareness to the internal or external things that trigger us to engage in disordered behaviours means that either we can put things in place to avoid the trigger [for example if we know going food shopping on an empty stomach is a trigger, we can ensure we eat a meal or snack close to a shopping trip]; or we can use our skills to change our response to the trigger.

A trigger may be something external such as walking past a shop, seeing a reflection in the mirror or noticing something on social media, or it may be internal such as a feel, sensation or memory. It is important to bring awareness to triggers without judgement as this these lead to an unconscious thought/feeling or sensation which leads to the behaviour we are trying to prevent which has consequences.

Trigger -> feeling/thought/sensation -> behaviour -> consequence.

31

To start to recognise triggers it may be beneficial to keep a journal to reflect on moments where we have leaned on disordered behaviours or avoided behaviours that would be positive for us. This way we can start to see any patterns and empower ourselves to start to make changes.

RULES OF LIVING AND CORE BELIEFS

Core beliefs are a person's most central ideas about themselves, others, and the world. These beliefs act like a lens through which every situation and life experience is seen. Because of this, people with different core beliefs might be in the same situation, but think, feel, and behave very differently.

These ideas develop during childhood as we begin to use our relationships with caregivers and our own experience to interpret the world around us. From this learning and interpretation, we develop specific thoughts and rules that allow us to get our needs met. While in many cases these beliefs can be helpful, there are times when they can cause negative emotions. For example, it is has been suggested that those individuals who experience symptoms of depression are more likely to have core beliefs that tell them that they are helpless and/or unloveable.

One technique to identify core beliefs uses our automatic thoughts, which we can notice if we pay attention to the thoughts bouncing around our minds all day. The downward arrow technique asks us to begin to ask questions about our automatic thoughts. Here are some questions that can be helpful:
1. What does this statement say about me in this situation? What does it mean?
2. What does this thought tell me or say about how I view the world, my friends or my family?
3. What is the worst thing that this statement or thought may say? Why is this situation, thought or feeling so bad?
4. What thoughts do I have about myself that would make this thought or situation so bad? What is causing me to feel so upset?

A rule for living is the behavioural adjustment that we may make in order to cope with negative messages that we have internalised about ourselves as a result of experiences and to align with our core beliefs.

For example:
I need to be X amount of weight to be able to wear a bikini.
I should keep working even when I am exhausted if I want to get ahead
If I don't try then I won't fail

SIGNIFICANT EARLY EXPERIENCES

It can be hugely beneficial to gently review your experiences in order to accept them and understand how they may have had an impact on thoughts, feelings and behaviours in the present day. It can be useful to draw two timelines, a life experiences timeline and an eating behaviours/exercise/body image time line and then reflect on them both together to see if anything aligns and offers greater understanding. It is important to lean on safety resources when doing this as it can be distressing.

TIMELINE ONE: LIFE

BIRTH

TIMELINE TWO: EATING BEHAVIOURS

Aged four: parents divorced - spent alot of time with nanny as this felt safe and loving.

Nanny used to bake cakes and allow me to have as much as I wanted, mum only gave us a treat on a Friday, she was cross about all the sugary foods and so I used to pretend we didn't eat it.

Aged 10: Started dance more seriously, was known as the "big girl" because I was so tall.

Restriction started lost a lot of weight and was praised for it. Couldn't stick to it so would sometimes buy a cinnamon bun and eat it in the woods. Felt so guilty afterwards.

Aged 12: Dad got married and they had another baby, he didnt make much effort with us.

Aegd 13: Nanny died.

Became obsessed with baking for others, but soon I was eating it all. Attempted to throw up but unable to. Continued to binge eat and restrict for about a year.

Aged 18: moved to university and loved it, but would home every weekend as was worried about leaving mum.

Eating behaviours got slightly better for a short time.

Aged 22: got a new job in a different country

Started weight watchers after comments from mum about weight gain and her concern for health. Lost weight for six months but regained it.

PRESENT DAY

TIMELINE ONE LIFE: TIMELINE TWO EATING BEHAVIOURS:

BIRTH

PRESENT DAY

PART 3: EXERCISE 1

Tune into your body in this moment. Describe what you are experiencing. You can use these descriptors to help describe sensations;

Texture : flat, dull , rough, firm, soft, smooth, fuzzy
Weight: heavy, light, spacious, cramped, dense, deep
Pain: deep, sharp, intense, subtle, ache, chronic, consistent, irregular, moving, burning, prickly, electric
Pace: quick, slow, stagnant, strong, rapid
Temperature: hot, cold, warm, chilly, damp, frosty, clammy, airy
Vibration: tingly, fuzzy, slow, shaky, smooth, pounding, irregular
Size: tiny, small, little, giant, big, in front, behind, next to, all consuming, taking over
Colour: red, yellow, black, multi colour, the colour of sky

From this exploration what state do you think your nervous system is in?

EXERCISE 2

What are you missing out on as a result of the disordered eating and exercise?

What is one thing you can do this week this week leaning on your safety resources that you have been to anxious to do in the past?

EXERCISE 3

What are your core beliefs and in what ways have you developed rules for living?

EXERCISE 4

What cognitive distortions have you noticed yourself using?

Can you reframe that thought so it is more accurate and helpful? Try to come up with three examples.

What have you noticed between your life experiences in relation to your eating and exercise behaviours?

How does it feel understanding this link?

The aim of formulating is to bring greater understanding and acceptance to why we continue to perform the behaviours we do. Looking back at the past is never about blame but about learning and accepting.

PART 4: INTRODUCTION:

Delving a little deeper into the basic understandings of the brain and its connection to the nervous system and body can offer more insight into the science behind why we may turn to behaviours that may not be optimal for our physical or mental health as well as see our body image inaccurately.

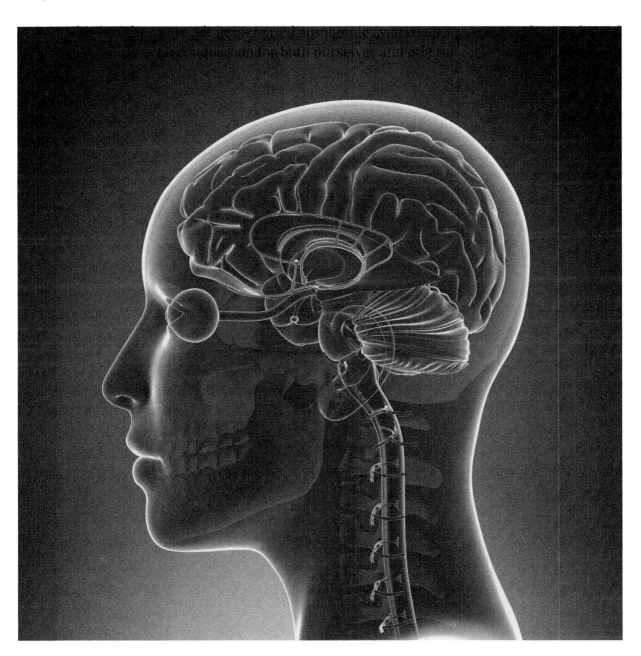

It consists of different parts including:

Thalamus - roles include regulation of sleep, alertness and wakefulness

Hypothalamus - roles include regulation of body temperature, hunger, fatigue and metabolic processes in general.

Hippocampus - responsible for long term memory formation and retrieval of memories

Amygdala - Major role is to process emotions, detection of threat and activation of appropriate fear-related behaviours in response to threatening or dangerous stimuli

When the AMYGDALA is triggered by sense of threat it interacts with the HIPPOCAMPUS and will send a message to the HYPOTHALAMUS which activates the limbic system and creates sympathetic activation in the nervous system. Recall that sympathetic = speed up (fight and flight). When the limbic system is activated it cannot properly pick up signals from the body and these shut down to aid survival. This may be why hunger and satiety cannot be felt during times of stress, anxiety or overwhelm.

For example, if we have fear food placed in front of us we may experience high levels of anxiety that is experienced as increased heart rate, shallow breathing, digestive issues and clammy hands. In the brain the threat detector (Amygdala) will talk with the memory centre [hippocampus] which has inaccurately stored that this food is a threat to survival and it will activate the hypothalamus to cause the physiological responses, in an attempt to get us to move away from or fight the threat. This is why we may experience very real pain or sensations in the body, without having anything physically wrong. A common example of this is fear of lactose triggering a physical reaction and we think we have a lactose intolerance so restrict this.

The behaviours we perform when our nervous system has been activated e.g. restriction can continue to activate the nervous system and often make us feel "crazy".

The way we see the body is determined by our nervous system state.

The parietal lobe which is in the forebrain is where body image and perception live. If there is sympathetic activation e.g. fight or flight, the messages to the parietal lobe get distorted and body image is experienced inaccurately and distorted thoughts increase.

Food restriction is seen as a threat to survival and therefore activates sympathetic activation which is why when dieting or experiencing a restrictive eating disorder, negative thoughts around the body increase. When energy is restored to a healthy level, body image thoughts decrease.

On the opposing side when there is parasympathetic activation (safe and connected) there are much fewer thoughts about body image. If you think of the last time you experienced joy (safe and connected) it is likely you didn't have many thoughts about the body at this time.

This is normally experienced when engaged in the present moment such as playing a game, water skiing or being creative.

There is another part of the brain, the insula which is important to mention; the insula is in the mid brain and it send signals to the limbic system from the body. Located within the insula is the ACC and this registers interoceptive awareness. Interoceptive awareness is the ability to identify, access, understand, and respond appropriately to the patterns of internal signals so acts as an internal regulator.

This area of the brain is also responsible for organising a sense of self, or who we are. When in a state of sympathetic activation the ACC is not activated and interoceptive awareness is not available. It is only available in ventral vagal [safe and connected] which is why we often cannot identify or respond to internal signals when we are stressed or restricting and why our sense of self may also be confused.

If we are able to identify the ANS state we are in and notice as it moves between states then we are able to respond with increased flexibility, avoiding disordered eating behaviours and increasing compassion for ourselves and others.

You may have heard of this as the body-mind connection. The ongoing flow of information from the body to the brain impacts the intensity of emotions and experiences. Research has shown that reduced autonomic awareness results in experiencing less positive moments and increased difficulty with making decisions. Resilience research has also suggested that individuals with low resilience have less awareness of autonomic states and are therefore less able to use physiological signals to support making decisions.

The goal is to develop awareness of both the subtle, nuanced changes in the way a state is experienced and expressed as well as the larger shifts in state.

ENHANCING ANS ATTUNEMENT

EXERCISE 4.1 AUTONOMIC NAME

In this exercise to experience your identity through different states. Using the letters in your first name, describe who you are in safe and connected, fight and flight and freeze states. Try writing several different variations as this can help you to see what stories emerge.
For example "RACHEL"

SAFE AND CONNECTED
 R: relaxed A: accepting C: connected H: happy E: energised L: loving
FIGHT AND FLIGHT
 R: raging A: anxious C: cross H: hostile E: envious L: looping
FREEZE:
 R: retracted A: absent C: collapsed H: hopeless E: exhausted L:lost

SAFE AND CONNECTED:

FIGHT AND FLIGHT:

FREEZE:

41

EXERCISE 2: SHORT STORIES

This is an exercise to add narrative to an experience as a way to connect body to mind and reflect on the way activation of the ANS begins the creation of stories. Spend no more than five minutes on writing each story using the prompts below and try to do this three times weekly.

My autonomic state is ...
 My system is responding to ...
 My body wants to ...
 My brain is making up a story that ...
When I review my short story I notice ...

Do this exercise now and then you will do it as 'homework' every week for the next few weeks.

EXERCISE 3: PIE CHARTS

This exercise is a visual representation of your day. We tend to give our days labels e.g. good day vs bad, busy day vs relaxed day based on one or two very intense moments. This exercise allows us to take a step back and reflect on the amount of time we spent within each state. Draw a blank circle at the end of each day and choose a different colour to represent each three states. Fill in your pie chart and then give the day a name. At the end of each week try to reflect on your autonomic experience over time. As we reshape the ANS we are hoping to see more of the colour for safe and connected on the pie chart.

Try to also reflect on whether there are any similarities. For example is there a day of the week that tends to be more fight or flight dominant? can you work out what triggers this?

How have you felt today if you were going to draw a pie chart? example below.

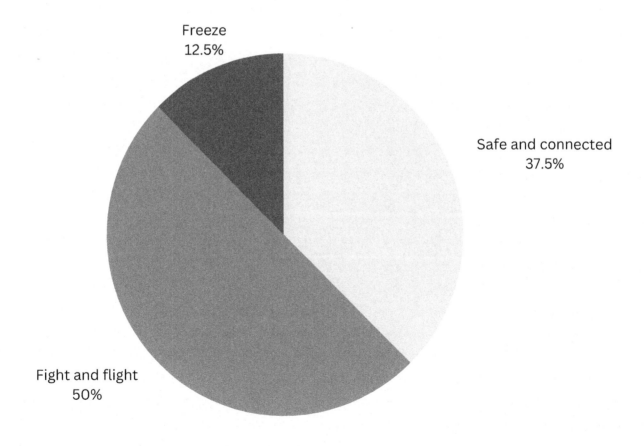

THE DRIVE FOR CONNECTION

The ANS is wired for connection by picking up signals of eyes, voice, faces and gestures; these are all cues to explore a relationship. Through our personal experiences, the nervous system has been shaped so invitations to connect may be misinterpreted.

The ANS is picking up signals from the muscles around the eyes, the wrinkles that express emotion, the tone and frequency of the voice. A moving face is a safe face. Tilting the head suggests safety and interest.

As you begin to understand how nervous systems communicate you can be aware of the cues you are sending and interpret more accurately the cues you are receiving which means being more skilled at navigating relationships.

Start to look into the eyes of others, listening to voices, observing facial expressions. Try to bring awareness to the present moment. Try to notice:
How their eyes are signalling
What their tone of voice sounds like?
What is their face is expressing?
What are their gestures are conveying?
Consider what characteristics are inviting connection or prompting a move into disconnection.
What part of their expression is signalling to your nervous system safety or danger?

CULTIVATING SELF COMPASSION

As we bring greater understanding to why we behave in the ways we do, we are able to reduce self identification with disordered eating and decrease feelings of shame. We can continue to nurture this through self kindness, common humanity and mindfulness which are the core components of self compassion. Some gentle ways to start to practise self compassion include;
Speak and treat yourself as you would a friend.
Be tender with yourself when you make a mistake.
Listen to your own needs such as putting yourself to bed at a reasonable time.
Remind yourself that everyone struggles and you are not alone.
Reach out to others for support.
Try to stop judging and comparing yourself.

Self compassion is important in the recovery of disordered eating as:

1. It allows recovery to be messy and non linear
2. It softens expectations by accepting it will be difficult
3. It is kinder, gentler and less harsh - swapping criticism in the tough moments for kindness
4. It embraces a holistic view - that it isn't just in the mind, nurturing mind, body and spirit is so important
5. It embraces understanding. This might mean there are tough moments because there is a new understanding of what needs to be recovered from
6. It embraces difficulties - out of darkness comes light
7. It reframes a relapse as an opportunity of rediscovery

EXERCISE 4:

When was the last time you experienced joy?

Did you experience any body image thoughts at this time?

Were you present in the moment?

PART 5:
BREATH PRACTICE

Breathing, thinking and feeling are tied together through the ANS.

Breath is an ANS process that occurs without consciousness and also breath can be consciously shaped. Intentional breath practise can induce a state of calm and regulation.

Extended exhales bring more safe and connection Short, sharp inhales bring more activation and upregulation.

We're going to do a few different breathing methods now. As we do each, make note of how it feels to you. Think about which one feels 'most right'.

Cocoa Breaths

Back body breathing

4:8

Box breathing

Three part breath

Finger breathing

Resistance is natural to experience during times of change, it can feel uncomfortable and we can use our safety resources to explore this in a beneficial and gentle way.

What behaviours are you struggling to change or desire to change?

Explore the resistance around this by visualising the change and the outcome.
What beliefs/circumstances are keeping you stuck?

What is an alternative viewpoint?

How can you use a more curious, non judgemental approach with this?

GOAL SETTING

Setting ourselves goals can be an important part of the healing process as this gives us something to aim for, and a measure of progress. It is important we make these behaviour-based rather than outcome based.

For example setting a goal of "I will not binge for six weeks" is an outcome goal; behavioural goals would be "I will follow eat the rainbow for four weeks by preparing doing my weekly shop online, preparing my breakfasts the night before and including a variety of snacks."

It is important we make a goal "SMART"
Specific
Measurable
Attainable
Realistic
Time bound

Note one goal down for the next four weeks.

GRIEF

As we start to feel safe enough to let go of distressing eating and exercise behaviours we can experience a sense of loss of something. This can create discomfort and suffering.

Allow yourself to feel, explore and express
Allow there to be anger and sadness, sit with it in safety.
How could you safely express these?
Nurture your past self like you would a friend, consider exploring "inner child work"

Share your experience of grief in a journal or with someone in your support network.

When we talk about "media" we mean the TV programs we watch, the social media we consume, the newspapers we read, the advertising we are exposed to, the books we read, the music we listen to, the games we play and so much more.

Media are designed to create a response within us; and therefore all types of media can have an impact on our nervous system and thus our feelings, thoughts and behaviours. Gaining greater understanding of how the media work empowers us to be able to navigate them skilfully, avoid aspects that can be harmful and use distress tolerance skills when we cannot avoid something that might be triggering and potentially lead to engaging in disordered behaviours.

MEDIA LITERACY

Media literacy is the the ability to interpret and create personal meaning from the thousands of verbal and visual symbols we take in everyday through television, radio, computers, newspapers, magazines, and advertising. It's the ability to choose and select, the ability to challenge and question, the ability to be conscious about what's going on around us and not be passive and therefore, vulnerable.

Media literacy has become critical in the modern age so we can control the interpretation of what we want to see and hear, rather than allow media to control us. Media literacy is a skill that is always evolving. It is not about memorising facts or statistics, but rather to be curious, to question and to inquire.

We can use a technique called Action Learning to enhance media literacy, which can be summarised as a four-step "empowerment" process: Awareness, Analysis, Reflection and Action. This involves observing a medium of choice, questioning it using the core questions on the next page, reflecting on how this impacts our own lives and actioning changes to support our own wellbeing.

When viewing any media it is important we ask ourselves some core questions.

1. Who created this message?
Whoever created this media has made choices based on what to include, enhance or remove based on their own goals and belief system. Are they trying to sell something? If so, consider how the media itself may not be real.

2. What techniques have been used to construct this message?
Camera angles? Photoshop? Lighting? Sound? Computer editing? Celebrity endorsements? Visuals? Filters? Remember that even a selfie taken from a phone camera have be hugely altered and that a single image is not what someone looks like every day.

3. What lifestyles, values and beliefs are shown or left out from this message?
From advertisements to social media, the user will have an intention to posting. What do you think their values are in the message? Think about the meaning behind the message, what has been included or left out. Does the individual showing a lean physique talk about the sacrifices they made to their social, mental and emotional health to get that physique?

4. How might someone else understand the same message?
We interpret messages based on our own individual skill level and belief system as well as our personal experiences. Different people may have different views about fatness or thinness and the media can perpetuate these. Ask yourself what the message means to you and how it impacts your body satisfaction, does it make you want to do or change anything?

5. What is the purpose of the message?
Is it to sell something? Do you think the advertiser is trying to get you to feel negative about yourself and their product to be the answer? Remember that the media are a business and the goal is to make money, they do this by selling our attention to advertisers. The bigger the audience the bigger the profit.

Consider who is paying for your attention? Is it something you want to support?

When we develop increased awareness of the state of our system, we are able to identify when it changes and can notice the triggers that created that state change. We can use our knowledge of our own internal state and our increased media literacy to support ourselves to choose media that does not lead to dysregulation; and also to bring ourselves back to a regulated place prior to any media we do consume. This supports us to use healthy ways to cope, instead of turning to impulsive and/or disordered behaviours.

For example, becoming dysregulated around a media trigger may look like: immediately purchasing something after it being advertised; calculating a week's food intake on a calorie counter after scrolling social media and seeing lots of lean bodies; eating a packet of popcorn after watching something sad on the TV; or skipping dinner after seeing an advertisement with slim women in.

Learning to regulate and then ask core questions about the media being consumed means that we are media conscious, we are aware of what may be triggering and can choose to avoid this completely, or move towards it and lean on our safety resources.

GRADED EXPOSURE

We cannot always avoid media triggers as we swim in a sea of media; therefore it is important that when we have safety resources firmly established, we move towards these triggers in a structured and safe way; this means that we won't experience excess activation or dysregulation when we do come face to face with them; and if we do, we know how to tolerate this without turning to destructive behaviours.

EXERCISE 6.1: GRADED EXPOSURE PLAN

STEP ONE: Create honest and non-judgemental awareness around what your media triggers are. These are the things that you notice a change in your physiological sensations e.g. faster heart rate, clammy hands; or a change in your thoughts e.g. I need to lose weight, or a change in your behaviour e.g. skipping dinner, as a result of the media you have consumed.
In this example we will use seeing fitness influencers on social media. (Although it is beneficial to unfollow them, it is also impossible to avoid them completely so we want to learn that we have the skills that if they pop up on something we are scrolling, we are able to navigate that experience safely.)

Who do you need to unfollow?

STEP TWO: Create your safety resources for approaching that situation e.g.
1. ground your feet to the floor
2. take three deep extended exhale breaths
3. have a warm cup of tea
4. open the jaw and relax the shoulders away from the ears.

STEP THREE: Create belief reframes to make these beliefs more neutral and rational. e.g. "These fitness influencers are more than their bodies, they are living, feeling people with emotions." "These photos are just one time point at one angle and not a reflection of what bodies look like day to day." "Leanness does not equate to health."

STEP FOUR: Visualise yourself scrolling social media and seeing lean fitness influencers. Observe any state changes and use your safety resources to let your system know that you are safe. Repeat your new reframed beliefs.

EXERCISE 2

How skilled do you feel in media literacy?

What is one thing you would benefit from focusing on to enhance your skill set?

EXERCISE 3

When you are scrolling social media what state are you often in? Ventral vagal? Sympathetic? Dorsal vagal?

What does looking at images of food or bodies do to the state of your system?

What are five things in the media that you are currently exposed to that impact you in a negative way? e.g. adverts with slim females in.

How do they impact you e.g. thoughts, feelings, sensations, behaviours

EXERCISE 4

Explore in detail one time that you felt triggered / a change of state to something in the media. Recall what happened as a result of that trigger and what was the consequence of this?

The aim of understanding media and its impact on the nervous system and thus eating behaviours, is to be able to create change in both the media we consume and also the way we respond to media with more insight and rational.

54

Once we are able to identify the different states that our system is in, we then often realise that we spend time in intense mobilisation (fight and flight) and withdrawal (freeze). This occurs when the state of safety is missing as the ANS has been acting in service of survival due to its experiences. Remember that the ANS works by habituation, which is why one person may be afraid of dogs (danger threat due to watching a film about a scary dog when younger) and another may love dogs and find them a safe place.

There are daily practices that we can introduce to reshape the nervous system towards safety and connection and expand our window of tolerance so we spend more time in our ventral vagal state. This is the state where we are grounded, open, relaxed, engaged and regulated.

COMFORT ZONE

When introducing new activities or interventions we do not want to stress the nervous system and create a survival response, but rather we want to stretch its capacity. To reshape our ANS towards safety we want to notice when it is in a state of safety and connection and celebrate it to deepen the experience; if our system is generally in fight or flight, we want to create intentional releases of energy to create new pathways; if we tend to live in freeze state we want to gently increase sympathetic mobilisation to create new patterns.

We can use different resources to try and build ways to move up to safety and connection and stay there which means we do not need to to turn to disordered behaviours. It can be trial and error as we learn what resource we have and how much we need to lean on it to create safety in the system, so it is important to take a curious, non judgemental approach.

GLIMMERS AND GLOWS

Glimmers are micro-moments of ventral vagal (safety and connection) that appear in your everyday life yet often go unnoticed. To support survival humans are born with a negativity bias so it is normal to pay more attention to negative events. Noticing the moments of regulation amongst the chaos is vital to expanding experiences of safety and connection; this helps to find more moments of safety.

1.Set an intention to look for a certain number of glimmers each day.

2.Notice when you feel a spark of ventral vagal energy. These glimmers happen regularly but you need to look for them.

3.See, stop and appreciate your glimmers. Create a way to acknowledge a glimmer. You may say silently "hello glimmer" or perhaps place your hand on your heart.

4.On your phone or in your journal try and track your glimmers.

5.Look for glimmers in specific places or with specific people.

6.Share your glimmers with others.

When we have become confident in noticing the glimmers we can create a more expansive experience of safety and connection, "glows".

1.Notice a glimmer and stop and let it fill you. Stay with the experience for at least 30 seconds.

2.Feel what happens when you move from connecting to a micro moment to a longer moment.

3.Listen to the story that comes along with the glow.

4.Describe your experience of a glimmer and a glow.

Prosody is the rhythm and pitch of the voice. This changes depending on our state. If we are hyper aroused we are likely to speak in a higher pitch at a faster rate; where as if we are hypo-aroused, our voice may sound monotone. Our nervous system picks up from others whether they are safe or a threat.

1.Try telling yourself a story in differing tones of voice; see if it creates a change in your system.

2.Try talking to your partner or friend in a different tone of voice. See if they receive it differently.

3.Try picking up voice cues from others when they talking to see if you can notice the state they are in.

When listening to music we can notice a change in our state. Our heartbeat, breath and cognitions often synchronise with the music which makes it an autonomic regulator. Music is a way to create safety and engagement in both dorsal (freeze) and sympathetic (fight/flight) states.

Take an inventory of the role that music plays in your life: Do you listen to music?

Do you hear music live?

Do you have a favourite radio station?

57

How much music is in your everyday life?

Is there enough music in your everyday experience?

How is music a regulating resource?

How can you add more musical moments?

What pieces of music can take you to different states?

MOVEMENT

Movement has the power to move us emotionally and mentally; when we notice something move out of the corner of our eye it makes us turn to look at it, whether a flickering flame from a candle, a feather blowing in the wind or a bird flying overhead. Movement gives us the feeling that something is alive nearby, the sense of aliveness.

The ability to turn inwards towards the body's sensations as we move is therapeutic; research shows that not only moving the body, but bringing movement to life in our mind's eye can create activation in the nervous system.

Movement exists along a continuum, simple to complex, micro to our entire body.

Unconscious movement can give us cues to our state. For example tapping our foot may show us that we have anxious energy to be discharged (hyperarousal); we can also use intentional movement to make hyperarousal and hypoarousal states feel less intense and more tolerable, as well as increasing the capacity to maintain a state of regulation.

By creating personal "movement lines" we can use movement to navigate each state. This is a trial and error process.

For each autonomic state create a continuum. At the end of each continuum write down an activity that you could utilise in that state that takes little energy to engage in.

At the other end of the continuum write an activity that you could engage in that takes a lot of energy.

In between these ends note down other activities that could decrease the intensity of hyper/hypo arousal or deepen the experience of safety.

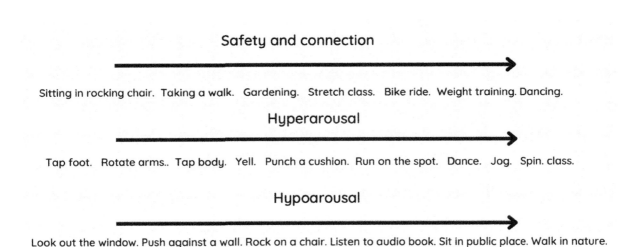

Safety and connection

Sitting in rocking chair. Taking a walk. Gardening. Stretch class. Bike ride. Weight training. Dancing.

Hyperarousal

Tap foot. Rotate arms.. Tap body. Yell. Punch a cushion. Run on the spot. Dance. Jog. Spin. class.

Hypoarousal

Look out the window. Push against a wall. Rock on a chair. Listen to audio book. Sit in public place. Walk in nature.

IMAGINED ACTION

Depending on personal and environmental circumstances it is not always possible to actually engage in moving the body; this is where visualisation can come into use. This can also be beneficial if actual movement may feel too unsafe to begin with. Sometimes movement can trigger a protection response.

1.Think about a movement that you thought or spoke about doing but have not yet actioned (dancing or shaking or yogi heart openers are common ones). Bring this movement into your mind's eye, visualise yourself performing the movement.

2.Bring your awareness to the sensations you are experiencing as you bring this into your mind's eye. How are you feeling? What thoughts are coming up for you?

Take a moment every day to bring this movement to mind and notice if over time the imagined movement brings you closer to performing the movement.

60

Nature nurtures the nervous system. Research shows that nature contributes to resilience and is associated with feelings of safety. If getting out into nature feels too tough, research has found the looking at nature photos can create regulation after a period of distress. We could also find ways to bring nature to us; for example we could look after houseplants or have a bunch of beautiful flowers on the table.

Connecting with any form of nature is a restorative experience that brings us closer to safety and connection. Creating a habit of exploring nature can support us to maintain an ongoing relationship with nature and deepen our capacity in ventral vagal state.

Here are some ideas to connect more deeply with nature:
Spend time exploring the natural green spaces around you.
Explore the difference that happens when you immerse in warm and cold water.
Make physical connection to nature e.g. walk barefoot on earth, dig in soil with your hands, feel the texture of pebbles on the beach, dip your toes in the sea. Add a plant to your home or office space
Observe the sensations that happen as you smell freshly cut grass or rain. Introduce natural scents such as lavender, rose and bergamot in body creams, candles or oils.
 Look out the window at nature for at least five minutes or look at photos of nature for at least five minutes daily.

It is also important that we shape our home space so that it feels safe and connecting and a restorative place to spend time in. To do this try to tune into your body and notice:

As you look around your home, what objects or spaces create activation or depression in your system?

What creates unease?

As you look around your home, what feels safe, comforting, cosy and connecting?

What makes them feel this way?

What small changes you could make in your home and work place, or in a space in either that creates more safety and connection for you?

SHAPING THROUGH WRITING

Writing has a unique way to connect us to our feelings and thoughts. It has both long and short term regulating effects. Research has shown that writing about a past distressing experience can decrease the distress felt when thinking about the experience.
Regular reflecting on times of safety and of dysregulation are both important to bring awareness to states and reshape to a place of safety.

1.Set up a weekly reflection practise noting down experiences of safety and connection, as well as moments of dysregulation.

2.Create awareness of what happens in the body as you write about these experiences.

3.Find a safe person or coach to share your experiences with, telling our stories in safe places with safe people can be transformative.

Now safety resources have been developed and defined, although they will continue to expand and grow, we can start to explore play and peaceful solitude which are often neglected when we are in the midst of disordered eating.

Not only are these things often inaccessible when in a state of survival - as naturally the brain and body won't be promoting play when you are chased by a tiger - but they are also foundational to accessing more safety and connection.

The more safe we are, the more we play and spend time in solitude, and the more time we play and spend time in solitude, the more safe we feel. The more safety, play and peaceful solitude we let into our lives the more disordered behaviours will lessen.

EXPLORING PLAY

To play is a fairly difficult experience for many people. If we have been in a state of protection for a long time (there are lots of danger cues and not enough safety cues) the ANS will remain on guard and play will feel like an unsafe and pointless choice. Play involves staying in the safety or ventral vagal and harnessing the sympathetic activation of hyperarousal/fight or flight. So we can start to practise expanding our window of tolerance to feel safe experiencing some hyperarousal.

We can be playful by ourselves and also with others. Research shows us that when we can harness the power of play we are more resilient and can cope with increased adversity. Playfulness is not a luxury, but an everyday experience.

Here are some ideas to explore;
Identify when, where and with whom you feel the most playful.

63

Try noticing what the "inner critic" (Sh*t FM) is saying when you consider playing. Reframe this thoughts so they are more helpful and accurate.
What type of play did you enjoy as a child?

What type of play did you enjoy as a child?

Play, or Feeding Your Fairy as I often refer to it, can be as simple as some friendly banter with a friend or sharing a moment of laughter, but it can also be:
Riding your bike
Baking a cake
Dancing with family
Sewing
Swinging on a swing
Getting involved with sports
Painting
Video games
Board game
Escape room

EXPLORING SOLITUDE

Even though connection is important for us as human, we often have a desire to cultivate our inner world by spending time alone. This times allows to become more aware of feelings and impulses. Research has shown that solitude has a deactivating response on hyperarousal and creates a sense of restoration and calm.

Some people find it true that "absence makes the heart grow fonder" and find that they feel more connected to people after spending time in solitude; others report their connection blossoms.

If being alone is unfamiliar it can often feel like a danger threat which is why it is important to integrate it slowly into our everyday experience; solitude is often accompanied by stillness for example during traditional meditation. This is the safety and connection pathway meeting the freeze pathway so it can take practise to expand the tolerance window so this level of immobilisation feels safe. It may be beneficial to start meditation practise doing a walking meditation.

Solitude is not the same as loneliness. It is important to become attuned to how solitude feels.

Try and explore
How do loneliness and solitude feel different? Consider the three states?

Explore where in your daily environment you experience solitude.e.g. nature

Explore where in your daily experience you find solitude?

Where could you visit to gain the benefits of solitude.

Solitude does not have to be experienced by yourself although it often is, it is a state of being. Try to explore:
Where are the places you visit every day that are full of people that can provide solitude e.g. coffee shop.

Continue to explore solitude:
Try to consider what happens when you have a desire for solitude, think about the people you spend time with, your environment and the amount of requests on your time.

How much solitude do you need daily? Weekly?

How can you tell when you have had enough solitude?

EXPLORING REST AND STILLNESS

Rest in the form of stillness is so important to restore; just like loneliness, if rest feels unfamiliar it can feel like a danger threat and trigger a survival response. This means that rest doesn't feel calming, but rather anxiety inducing. If that happens we need to a moment to explore these sensations, and as we do it generally regulates our system

Try to explore
Notice restless and restful environments and create a continuum, filling out the environments in between that feel slightly restful.

Consider what about the spaces feel restful or restless.

What qualities feel restful and where can you find them easily?

What could you change with one area of your home to make it more restful ?

CONNECTING TO NATURE AND ART

Looking at how the world around us can provide safety resources if we seek them is a beneficial way to expand our safety toolbox. Both art and nature offer us ways to expand our state of safety and connection.

Nature in real life and through images and sounds can offer us relaxation and restoration; an idea of why this is is because nature offers fractals. These are patterns that repeat over and over. Imagine a leaf, pinecone, crystals or clouds; these have been found to bring regulation to the system.

Try to explore the natural world around you and;
Notice what happens to your body when you spend time in nature. Look for fractals as you move throughout your day.

Ensure you have fractals easily accessible eg. flowers on your desk, natural screensaver .

Looking at art supports us to see the world in a new way; it involves both the mind and the body. Engaging with art activates the safety and connection system and helps expand the window of tolerance. Finding ways to invite art into our daily lives can help us feel more regulated.

Try to explore
How is art available to you?

What kind of art are you attracted to?

How can you create in a regular way with art?

The autonomic nervous system learns through habituation. This means experiences, both negative and positive have the power to change what it does and does not respond to. When we relate this to eating behaviours, we realise that at one point these behaviours were adaptive and functional and supported us to manage a time that may have felt consciously or unconsciously unmanageable.

By attuning to the body and reshaping the nervous system we are able to prevent it from habitually turning to disordered behaviours during times of distress or discomfort and instead to tolerate the distress and/or choose to lean on safety resources.

When this is practised again and again, over time autonomic patterns begin to change. However before this there is a middle ground of not automatically turning to disordered eating behaviours, but also not having developed strongly established automatic behaviours. This can feel unfamiliar; this is where integration happens to develop new stories.

CONSOLIDATION

Consolidation is the process of making something stronger; in the process of recovery from disordered eating this looks like moving towards a life free from these behaviours even when we are feeling the physiological symptoms of anxiety or fear such as a fast heart rate, clammy hands, short sharp breathing. We all see the world through the state of our nervous system; we understand the link between autonomic state and emotional regulation; and both are dependant on attuning to the body; or in other words, knowing which state you are in.

Below are some exercises to continue to practise to integrate attunement, regulation and tolerance skills.

Exercise one:
1.Observe. Bring awareness to your current autonomic state.
 2.Try to name the state you are in depending what theory you are more aligned to. (Polyvagal/Window of Tolerance)

 3.Recognise any thoughts, feelings and behavioural urges you have in this state.

4.Avoid judgement and greet whatever state with compassion.
5.Repeat this often.

Exercise two:
1.Start to get curious about the "trigger" to any change in state e.g. what created movement into fight and flight?

What safety cues allowed you to experience safety?

2.What is the state you are in telling you?

What message does it want you to know?

3.Spend one minute trying to explore this message.

Exercise three:
1.Start to think about positive changes you want to happen around your autonomic flexibility.
2.Thinking about your current responses, what do you want to change or deepen in your autonomic response? For example, I want to feel safer when my partner cooks for me, or when chocolate is in the office.

Set some small intentions to support this e.g. I intend to use breath practise and grounding when my partner cooks, I intend to use visualisation about navigating going into the office and eating chocolate.

GOAL SETTING AND ACTION
Once you have identified the goals you want to explore, try to create some conditional statements, otherwise referred to as "if-then" statements. This is a plan to help you respond to a situation in a healthy way, which brings awareness between the triggers and the responses.

1.Set a goal for how you want to respond to a situation in each three states. Consider when, where and how. Using the sentence starter "If this happens then I will ..."

69

When writing these actions remember to push just to the edge of the comfort zone - too far and it will create a survival response. We want to stretch not stress the system to bring about change. Focus on the triggers which normally result in you engaging with a disordered eating behaviour.

e.g. If I am going to be around my family, I will make sure I eat before I go as they don't eat lunch.

If I am going out for dinner, I will ask for a healthy menu.

If I am hungry then I will eat something delicious and nutritious even if it is not a normal time.

If I notice that my heart is racing quickly without reason I will take three deep breaths.

If I notice myself feeling demotivated and disconnected I will splash my face with cold water and call a friend.

CREATING NEW PATHWAYS

If you imagine yourself in an overgrown field, there is one pathway which is clearly trodden down; you are familiar with this route and habitually walk down it; but you don't like where it is taking you. You therefore need to create another pathway. However this takes conscious effort, time and energy to tread down the long overgrown grasses to make a new pathway where you like the destination. Sometimes treading down the grasses is painful and challenging and sometimes you find yourself halfway down the old pathway; but each time you walk down the new pathway, the old pathway grows over a little bit, and a little bit more, until finally it is hardly recognisable.

Consider the ways your autonomic system is responding differently than previously. What examples can you give?

What state are you experiencing more or less of? How does life feel now you are more attuned?

RESILIENCE

Resilience happens when we have created greater safety resources than there are stressors or threats; this therefore makes resilience teachable with practise. We are able to notice we are not in a state of safety and bring ourselves back there if we don't need our nervous systems to protect us. We build this resilience as we complete cycles - from regulation to dysregulation and back to regulation. This is called pendulation.
Resilience helps us to remain confident in situations that provoke anxiety, to manage stress effectively and to experience the fear of change and not allow it to stop us.

Vagal break
The vagal break is the impact that the social engagement system has on the heart. When our ventral vagal or "safe and connected" pathway is activated our heart rate will be slower and overall stress level lower. When our vagal brake is strong, our daily life can be more manageable, our overall stress level is lower, and there is less perceived threat.

We can "press" the vagal break in a time of perceived stress to support ourselves return to a place of safety and connectedness. For some people it can be useful to create a "button" somewhere on the body e.g. the back of a hand, and visualise pressing this and thinking of something soothing or comforting such as the face of a loved one. After practice, each time we press the button we automatically visualise the face of a loved one or feel their presence and this creates a sense of regulation.

We can practise this by creating dysregulation in our system, for example listening to rock music and then pressing the break whilst using safety resources to return to regulation. We can repeat this in a process called pendulation.

RITUALS TO DEVELOP RESILIENCE

Building resilience practices into our daily lives expands our windows of tolerance: we won't turn to disordered behaviours when we are in a state of regulation and it also supports us to regulate after we have experienced a trigger.

Try to choose two different rituals, a core daily ritual which you maintain and another ritual which you change every few weeks to allow you to explore what feels good for you and expand your tool box.

For example:
Core ritual: four rounds of box breathing morning and evening, noticing glimmers and sending to a friend/journalling, meditating before bed.

Changing practises: hike every weekend, body scan daily, intentional sighing.

PART 10: INTRODUCTION

We know, especially after the pandemic, the extent to which our personal and communal wellbeing is impacted by isolation.

The social environment that we live in impacts our biology and has the power to switch on and off different genes.

When people feel disconnected they seem to have an increased inflammation response. We know that individuals experiencing distressing eating behaviours often feel more loneliness and isolation which can be a maintaining mechanism for staying stuck within this behavioural and feelings loop. Finding ways to connect and experience common humanity can be a transformative aspect of recovery.

CONNECTION

There is a human longing and biological need for connection. We enter the world wired for connection, and it is essential to our survival. We are taught self regulation via coregulation from our caregivers and then throughout our lives by the people around us.
We tend to connect with the people whose nervous system is in a similar state to our own as they feel familiar; or they may fit in with our own early life experiences.

As we bring more safety into our lives and "reshape" our systems towards more time in safety and connection, the people we are drawn to may also change, both friends and partners.
It is due to the state of our nervous system that we may interact with a lot of people and still feel lonely.

Connection seems to be a positive feedback loop. When are have deeper connections with friends and community, we are likely to have greater contentment and when we have greater contentment we are likely to have deeper connections. When we have greater contentment and deeper connections we are less likely to reach for disordered eating behaviours.

So our own contentment is somewhat impacted by the contentment of those in our social network.

EXPLORING CONNECTION

Reciprocity, Proximity and face to face interactions are all important for a sense of belonging.

Reciprocity: the practice of exchanging things with others for mutual benefit
Proximity: nearness in space
Face to face interactions: is social communication carried out without any mediating technology

We all require a certain amount of these and when our body senses that these needs are not being met it is seen as a threat and therefore primes the body for protection moving into arousal or fight, flight or freeze. However we need to find the balance between these and solitude, and our individual needs are all different for this.

We therefore need to know what our personal therapeutic daily dose of connection is and then build sustainable connections to meet these needs.

73

CONNECTION

It can take time to realise how much connection we need, but regular reflection can be a really important step to get to know your needs for solitude and connection.
We can write some connection intentions that list how we are going to pay attention to times that we are in or out of reciprocity.

The amount of time I want to spend alone today is ....

Today I am going to spend time alone doing ...

The amount of time I want to spend with friends/family is ...

Today I am going to connect with ....

We can also write some reciprocal intentions to identify when, where and with whom you can build predictable, sustainable connections into your life.

I have neglected being with the people in my life who are important to me by not paying attention to ...

I have been too busy with others I haven't made time for ...

I feel too involved in the life of...

CONNECTION REFLECTION

Creating a focused connection reflection can support us to find a way to create more connection in our lives.

When we do this plan, it can highlight where connection is missing in our lives which can feel like a threat and move us into a state of protection, which means we are unable to use our thinking, rational brain and explore, so lean on your safety anchors if you need to.

People I want to continue to spend time with

People I would like to explore a deeper connection with

Things I want to continue to explore with friends/family

Things I would like to explore doing with others

Things I want to keep doing to connect more deeply with myself

New things I would like to try

COMPASSION, AWE AND GRATITUDE

Compassion, awe and gratitude are all experiences that have the power to connect people. Connection enhances our experience of life and reduces the reliance of distressing eating behaviours.

Compassion is experienced in a state of safety and connection. When we feel safe we are able to see others' experience and respond compassionately. Both compassion and self compassion are strengthened the more we practise it.

75

Gratitude is an experience that enhances all areas of experiences, whether it's towards another, towards life itself or towards nature; as with everything practice deepens the gratitude response.

Awe is defined as something that is larger than yourself or beyond normal experience, and also the readjustment of ways of thinking to adjust to the new experience. It is something that reminds us there is something bigger than ourselves and that we are part of humankind.

GRATITUDE

Gratitude is often easier to experience than compassion or awe so this is always a good one to start with as a foundation for enhancing connection to something greater. The small acts we can do to express gratitude may include:

Keep a daily gratitude list
 Find ways to express gratitude daily
Make a purposeful point of telling your friends why you are grateful for them
Breath practice - breathe in a word that acknowledges what you are grateful for in this moment and breathe out a word that expresses your gratitude. For example breathing in family and breathing out deeply loved.

CONNECTING COMPASSIONATELY

When we are in a place of safety and regulation we are much more able to recognise another's dysregulation. This means we no longer see people as "bad" or "undeserving" but rather as "experiencing dysregulation/outside their window of tolerance."

We can also connect with our own suffering and respond with kindness when we are regulated. We can build up our capacity for compassion. Consider:

What are signs you recognise when someone else is dysregulated?

Write an affirmation that you can use when you see someone else who is experiencing dysregulation and then say this either aloud silently or send them a message e.g. I can see you are struggling and just wanted to let you know you mean a lot to me or I hope you know what a positive impact you make to my life.

To support someone else through co-regulation, try to notice dysregulation in another, then find your own safety anchor to ensure you are regulated before trying to hold that person in your ventral vagal energy and let your system be a cue of safety.

SELF COMPASSION AFFIRMATIONS

We can only access self compassion when we are in a state of safety. Compassion and safety form a feedback loop. When we are in a place of safety we expand our capacity for compassion and when we expand our capacity for compassion we expand our experiences of safety. When we are safe we will not desire turning to disordered behaviours.

To create affirmation to repeat in times of distress or discomfort;
Use language of the ANS
Acknowledge you are dysregulated and that this is a normal human experience
Acknowledge that your ANS will find its way back to regulation
Notice when you are in need of compassion and say your affirmations.

For example;
"I am noticing my body protecting me right now, I am in survival mode. This is normal to experience. I know my nervous system will find it's way back to safety if I breathe deeply and move gently. I am safe. "

AWE

Awe lives along a continuum from the ordinary to the extraordinary. Awe is defined as something that is larger than yourself or beyond normal experience. Being awe-filled makes us feel moved by an experience, awe-struck makes us feel unable to move.
It can be beneficial to reflect on our awe experiences:

Bring to mind an experience of being in awe - try and explore how that feels physiologically. Sometimes this can be hard to reflect on, perhaps watching the sunrise, noticing birds fly together, fireworks, seeing your friend walk down the isle, being in a concert, coming across a beautiful view.

77

Explore in your life where you experience awe. Perhaps some people inspire awe within you, places, art, music, nature, spiritual experiences.

Sometimes moments of awe are unexpected but they are also intentionally inspired e.g. going to watch a sunset. How can you bring more awe into your life?

Connecting invites us to explore the places, the experiences and the people that nourish our nervous systems. As we reshape our ANS we are able to stay in a place of regulation towards connection instead of dysregulating towards protection. This allows us to not need to use previous protective behaviours as we are more connected to ourselves, others and the world.

HOMEWORK

PIE CHART

How have you felt today? Draw lines in the circle to estimate what percentage of your day you have spent:
- Feeling safe and connected
- Fight or flight
- Freeze

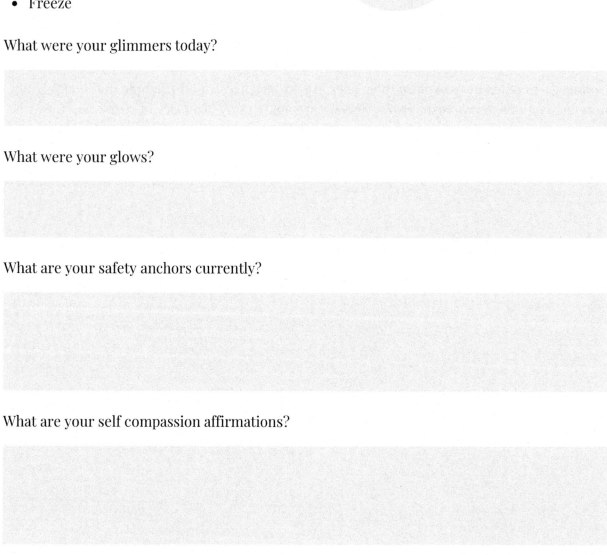

What were your glimmers today?

What were your glows?

What are your safety anchors currently?

What are your self compassion affirmations?

Homework

Start to develop your own formulation. Do this referring back to page 29

HOMEWORK

PIE CHART

How have you felt today? Draw lines in the
circle to estimate what percentage of your
day you have spent:
- Feeling safe and connected
- Fight or flight
- Freeze

What were your glimmers today?

What were your glows?

What are your safety anchors currently?

What are your self compassion affirmations?

HOMEWORK

Create your own graded exposure plan to something in the media that you find triggering. Ensure you have detailed your safety anchors. Use the one on pages 51-52 as reference.

Homework

PIE CHART

How have you felt today? Draw lines in the circle to estimate what percentage of your day you have spent:
- Feeling safe and connected
- Fight or flight
- Freeze

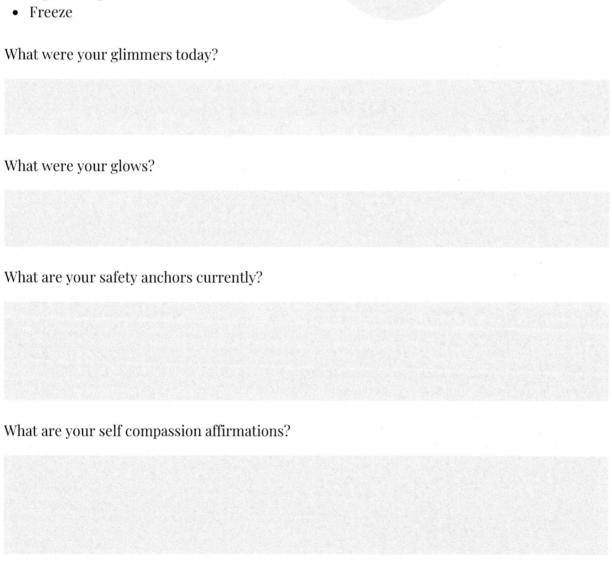

What were your glimmers today?

What were your glows?

What are your safety anchors currently?

What are your self compassion affirmations?

Homework

SHORT STORIES

This is an exercise to add narrative to an experience as a way to connect body to mind and reflect on the way activation of the ANS begins the creation of stories. Spend no more than five minutes on writing each story using the prompts below and try to do this three times weekly.

My autonomic state is ...
 My system is responding to ...
 My body wants to ...
 My brain is making up a story that ...
When I review my short story I notice ...

HOMEWORK

PIE CHART

How have you felt today? Draw lines in the
circle to estimate what percentage of your
day you have spent:
- Feeling safe and connected
- Fight or flight
- Freeze

What were your glimmers today?

What were your glows?

What are your safety anchors currently?

What are your self compassion affirmations?

Homework Journal

How I am feeling today about my body, food, and my emotions

HOMEWORK

PIE CHART

How have you felt today? Draw lines in the
circle to estimate what percentage of your
day you have spent:
- Feeling safe and connected
- Fight or flight
- Freeze

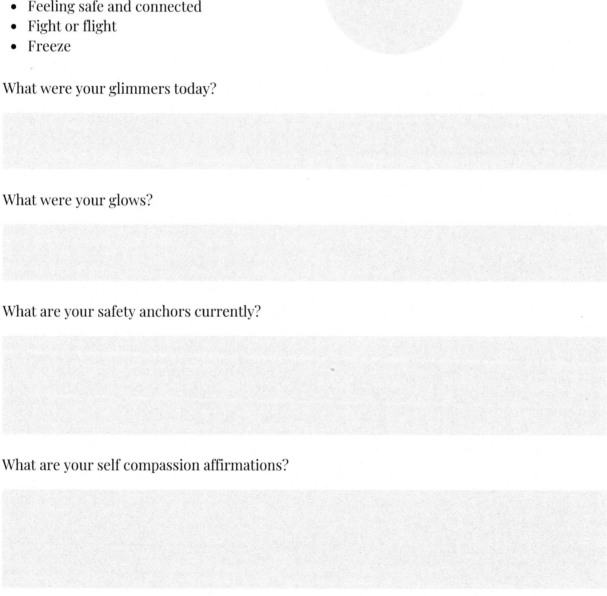

What were your glimmers today?

What were your glows?

What are your safety anchors currently?

What are your self compassion affirmations?

Homework Journal

How I am feeling today about my body, food, and my emotions

HOMEWORK

PIE CHART

How have you felt today? Draw lines in the
circle to estimate what percentage of your
day you have spent:
- Feeling safe and connected
- Fight or flight
- Freeze

What were your glimmers today?

What were your glows?

What are your safety anchors currently?

What are your self compassion affirmations?

HOMEWORK JOURNAL

How I am feeling today about my body, food, and my emotions

HOMEWORK

PIE CHART

How have you felt today? Draw lines in the circle to estimate what percentage of your day you have spent:

- Feeling safe and connected
- Fight or flight
- Freeze

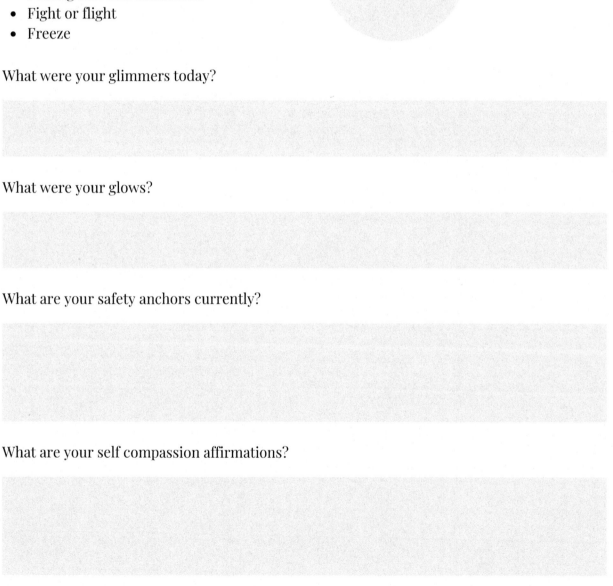

What were your glimmers today?

What were your glows?

What are your safety anchors currently?

What are your self compassion affirmations?

HOMEWORK JOURNAL

How I am feeling today about my body, food, and my emotions

MY THOUGHTS

MY THOUGHTS

MY THOUGHTS

MY THOUGHTS

MY THOUGHTS

MY THOUGHTS

MY THOUGHTS

MY THOUGHTS

NOTES

NOTES

NOTES

NOTES

NOTES

Printed in Great Britain
by Amazon